First World War
and Army of Occupation
War Diary
France, Belgium and Germany

57 DIVISION
172 Infantry Brigade
Prince of Wales's Volunteers (South Lancashire Regiment)
2/4th Battalion
2 September 1915 - 24 July 1916

WO95/2985/7

The Naval & Military Press Ltd
www.nmarchive.com
Published in association with The National Archives

Published by

The Naval & Military Press Ltd

Unit 10 Ridgewood Industrial Park,

Uckfield, East Sussex,

TN22 5QE England

Tel: +44 (0) 1825 749494

www.naval-military-press.com

www.nmarchive.com

This diary has been reprinted in facsimile from the original. Any imperfections are inevitably reproduced and the quality may fall short of modern type and cartographic standards.

© Crown Copyright
Images reproduced by permission of The National Archives, London, England, 2015.

Contents

Document type	Place/Title	Date From	Date To
Heading	WO95/2985/7 57 Divn 172 Inf Brig 2/4 5th Lancs Regt 1915 Sept 1916 Feb		
Heading	War Diary From 1st September, 1915 To 30th, September 1915.		
War Diary	Oxted Surrey	02/09/1915	30/09/1915
Heading	2/4th Battalion South Lancashire Regiment War Diary From October 1st 1915 To October 31st 1915		
War Diary	Oxted	02/10/1915	22/10/1915
War Diary	Seal	23/10/1915	23/10/1915
War Diary	Maidstone	24/10/1915	21/11/1915
Heading	War Diary And Summary Of Events And Information Headquarters 2/4th. Bn. South Lancs. Regiment. Period November 1st 1915 To November 30th 1915.		
Heading	War Diary From 1st November, To 30th November 1915		
War Diary	Maidstone	01/11/1915	28/11/1915
Heading	2/4th Battalion South Lancashire Regiment War Diary From:- 1st December 1915 To:-31st December 1915		
War Diary	Maidstone	01/12/1915	30/12/1915
Heading	2/4th Battalion South Lancashire Regiment War Diary From 1st January, 1916 To 31st January 1916.		
War Diary		03/01/1916	31/01/1916
Heading	War Diary Of 2/4th Battalion South Lancashire Regiment Period 1st February 1916 To 29th February 1916		
War Diary	Maidstone	07/07/1916	24/07/1916

WO 95 2985/7

57 Divn; 172 Inf. Brig
2/4 Sth. Lancs Regt
1915 Sept – 1916 Feb

WAR DIARY.

From

1st September, 1915 to
30th, September, 1915.

[signature] Lieut. Colonel,
                Commanding,
2/4th, Battalion South Lancs: Regiment.

Tandridge Camp,
    Oxted, Surrey,
        1st, October, 1915.

Army Form C. 2118.

WAR DIARY
or
INTELLIGENCE SUMMARY.
(Erase heading not required.)

Instructions regarding War Diaries and Intelligence Summaries are contained in F.S. Regs., Part II. and the Staff Manual respectively. Title pages will be prepared in manuscript.

Hour, Date, Place	Summary of Events and Information	Remarks and references to Appendices
Oxted Surrey Sept 2	Lt P.E.S. Hackett appointed acting Adjutant	
8	Rev. Father McGrath transferred to 25 Infantry Brigade	
9	2nd Lieut. E.D. Smith reported for duty	
11	Capt. J.P. Killick seconded vice Major H.W.W. Southey	
13	2nd Lieut. L. Brooks proceeded to School of Instruction at Cambridge	
16	2nd Lieut. Burgoyne & Seeds attached for training reported	
20	2nd Lieut. E.D. Smith proceeded to Bisley to undergo a course of Instruction Machine Gun	
30	Sergt. Davies proceeded to school of Instruction Chelsea	
	2nd Lieuts. Ashton, Beastow, Count Cheetle Clarkson attached to the battalion for training reported this arrival	
23	Rev. Father J.O. reported for duty with 172 Brigade attached to 2/4 Bn. South Lancs Regt.	
24	Lieut. Collingworth demobilised for a journal of three months	
27	Lieut. R. Putman proceeded to Bathcarpton for joni	
	1/4 Pm wasaing	
	2nd Lieut F.S. Jackson reported his arrival	
Hxy 21	2nd Lieut Ashton attached for training reported his arrival	
30	Brand of the battalion proceeded to Wandytor (according chalais)	

.... Lieut. Colonel,
Commanding
2/4 Bn. So. Lancashire Regiment.

2/4th BATTALION SOUTH LANCASHIRE REGIMENT.

WAR DIARY.

from October 1st, 1915
to October 31st, 1915.

[signature] Lieut-Colonel,
Commanding,
2/4th Battalion South Lancashire Regiment.

WAR DIARY
or
INTELLIGENCE SUMMARY. 2/4 Bn South Lancs. Regt

Army Form C. 2118.

(Erase heading not required.)

Hour, Date, Place	Summary of Events and Information	Remarks and references to Appendices
Oxted Oct. 2/15	2nd Lieut E.G. Linnell proceeded to Blackheath undergo course of Instruction Transport duties	
4	Lieut Purdy proceeded to Bisley Course of Musketry Instruction	
14	Sergt Briggs proceeded to Wrotham Pioneer Course	
21.	2nd Lieut Bell proceeded to Maidstone on Billeting duties	
22	The Battalion moved by route march from Oxted to Seal a distance of about 13½ miles. Departing Oxted 5 a.m. Arr. Seal 1-30.	
Seal. 23.	The Battalion moved by route march from Seal to Maidstone a distance of about 14 miles. Departed Seal 6 a.m. arrived Maidstone 1.10. The Battalion being billetted in furnished houses and messed Centrally	
Maidstone 24	Capt R.A. Fox proceeded to Royal Artillery College Camberley Course of Instruction	
25	2nd Lieut F.S. Jackson proceeded to Hulyad School of Instruction	
20.	45 Japanese .256 transferred to 44th Provisional Battalion	
21	40. D.P. 303 rifles transferred to C.O.O. Woolwich	

[signature] Lieut. Colonel,
Commanding
2/4 Bn. So. Lancashire Regiment.

WAR DIARY

and

SUMMARY OF EVENTS AND INFORMATION.

Headquarters
2/4th.Bn. South Lancs.Regiment.

PERIOD

November 1st 1915.

to

November 30th.1915.

8 Ashford Rd.
Maidstone
December 4th.1915

WAR DIARY
from
1st November, 1915, to 30th November, 1915.

Unit:- 2/4th BATTALION, SOUTH LANCASHIRE REGIMENT
BRIGADE:- 172nd INFANTRY BRIGADE.
Division:- 57th (WEST LANCASHIRE) DIVISION.
Mobilization Centre:- WARRINGTON.
Temporary War Station:- MAIDSTONE.
Stations since occupied:- BLACKPOOL; TUNBRIDGE WELLS; ASHFORD; OXTED, SURREY; MAIDSTONE.

Lieut-Colonel,
Commanding,
2/4th Battalion, South Lancashire Regiment.

WAR DIARY or INTELLIGENCE SUMMARY

Army Form C. 2118.

2/4 Bn South Lancs Regt.

Place	Date	Hour	Summary of Events and Information	Remarks and references to Appendices
Maidstone	Jan 1		Capt. Skinner proceeded to Chelsea Course of Instruction. 2nd Lieut Bell & 1 R.C.O. proceeded to Mytham Course of Grenade Instruction. 1 R.C.O. proceeded to attend Physical Training Course.	
	9		Capt. H.S. H. Davis R.A.M.C. proceeded to Ashford to take up duty with 140th Brigade. 2nd Lieut- A.B. Hurlin & 1 R.C.O. proceeded to Mytham to undergo a Pioneer Course.	
	15		1 R.C.O. proceeded to Dartford in Cookery Course. 2nd Lieut Jacob proceeded to Mytham to Mytham course in Trench warfare.	
	16		2 N Sergt & S.J. Price reported Lieutenants 9 Bn Lieut.	
	17		The Bn was inspected by F.O.C. 3Y West Lancs Division. Capt. R.S. Chudly attached 3Y West Lancs Division for special duty.	
	20		5/20 hrs Pattern (Japanese) Rifles despatched to 600 Woolwich. 5140. 303. rifles received at Read- 60% in bad condition.	
	23		1 R.C.O. proceeded to Sandridge Wells Signalling course.	
	24		Rev. E.N. Smith (Army & Navy Board) attached to the Battalion.	
	27		The Bn was inspected by Major Gen. E.S. Dickson Inspector 2nd Line Landinine Units.	
	28		28 Numbers of the Band transferred to 3/4 Bn South Lancs Regt.	

signature — Lieut. Colonel,
Commanding
2/4 Bn. So. Lancashire Regiment.

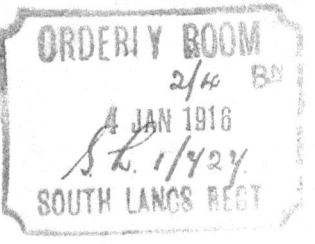

2/4TH BATTALION, SOUTH LANCASHIRE REGIMENT

WAR DIARY

From:- 1st December, 1915.
To:- 31st December, 1915.

                    Lieut-Colonel,
                        Commanding,
            2/4th Bn South Lancashire Regiment.

Army Form C. 2118.

WAR DIARY
or
INTELLIGENCE SUMMARY.
(Erase heading not required.)

Instructions regarding War Diaries and Intelligence Summaries are contained in F.S. Regs., Part II. and the Staff Manual respectively. Title pages will be prepared in manuscript.

Hour, Date, Place	Summary of Events and Information	Remarks and references to Appendices
MAIDSTONE Decr 1st 1915	2nd Lieutenant A.E.Newton proceeded to WROTHAM Pioneer Course.	
MAIDSTONE Dec 6th 1915	1 N.C.O. proceeded to BISLEY MUSKETRY COURSE.	
MAIDSTONE Dec 7th 1915	1 N.C.O. proceeded to WROTHAM INSTRUCTION IN TRENCH WARFARE.	
MAIDSTONE Dec 11th 1915	2nd Lieutenant G.Leak proceeded to SHREWSBURY - PAY DUTIES.	
MAIDSTONE Dec 13th 1915	2nd Lieut K.L.Gordon proceeded to WROTHAM - GRENADE COURSE.	
MAIDSTONE Dec 13th 1915	1 N.C.O. proceeded to BISLEY - MACHINE GUN COURSE.	
MAIDSTONE Dec 13th 1915	2 N.C.O's proceeded to DARTFORD - SCHOOL OF COOKERY.	
MAIDSTONE Dec 13th 1915	Inspection by G.O.C. 57th (WEST LANCASHIRE) DIVISION.	
MAIDSTONE Dec 14th 1915	Inspection by G.O.C. 2ND ARMY.	
MAIDSTONE Dec 27th 1915	Six 2nd Lieutenants promoted Lieutenants.	
MAIDSTONE Dec 30th 1915	Inspection by Commandant, School of Musketry, Hythe.	

Lieut-Colonel,
Commanding,
2/4th Battalion, South Lancashire Regiment.

2/4th Battalion South Lancashire Regiment

WAR DIARY

from 1st January, 1916.
To: 31st January, 1916.

[signature]
Lieut-Colonel,
Commanding,
2/4th Bn South Lancashire Regiment

Army Form C. 2118.

WAR DIARY
or
INTELLIGENCE SUMMARY.
(Erase heading not required.)

Instructions regarding War Diaries and Intelligence Summaries are contained in F.S. Regs., Part II. and the Staff Manual respectively. Title pages will be prepared in manuscript.

Hour, Date, Place	Summary of Events and Information	Remarks and references to Appendices
3rd January, 1916	3 N.C.O's to TUNBRIDGE WELLS – Course of Instruction.	
4th January, 1916	1 Private to TONBRIDGE – Course of Instruction in Saddlery.	
5th January, 1916	1 Officer to WREXHAM – Pioneer Course.	
10th January, 1916	5 Officers & 1 N.C.O. to WREXHAM – Trench Warfare Course.	
	1 N.C.O. to ENFIELD LOCK – Instruction in Repairs to Small Arms.	
11th January, 1916	2nd Lieut W.J. Brown posted to the Battalion from Territorial Force Reserve.	
21st January, 1916	23 Recruits – Derby Group Recruits – received from Admin.Centre, Warrington.	
22nd January, 1916	12 Recruits – Derby Group Recruits – received from Admin.Centre, Warrington.	
24th January, 1916	2nd Lieut C.D. Smith & W.J. Brown to WREXHAM – Trench Warfare Course.	
	Lieut G. Collingwood struck off strength of Battn & posted to 3/4th Bn S.L.Regt.	
	20 Recruits – Derby Group Recruits – received from Admin.Centre, Warrington.	
25th January, 1916	25 men transferred to 49th Provisional Battalion.	
26th January, 1916	23 Recruits – Derby Group Recruits – received from Admin.Centre, Warrington.	
27th January, 1916	4 Recruits – Derby Group Recruits – received from Admin.Centre, Warrington.	
	3 Recruits – Derby Group Recruits – received from Admin.Centre, Warrington.	
	Captain R.A. Fox to CANTERBURY – Field Training.	
28th January, 1916	2nd Lieuts J. Brookes & P.N. Ashton to WREXHAM – Pioneer Course.	
31st January, 1916	2nd Lieut C.E. Clarkson to WREXHAM – Pioneer Course.	
	Lieut F.H. Breedy to CANTERBURY – Field Training.	

Lieut. Colonel,
Commanding
3/4 Bn. So. Lancashire Regiment.

WAR DIARY

of

2/4TH BATTALION SOUTH LANCASHIRE REGIMENT

Period
1st February 1916 to 29th February 1916

Maidstone

8th March 1916

Army Form C. 2118.

WAR DIARY
or
INTELLIGENCE SUMMARY.
(Erase heading not required.)

Place	Date	Hour	Summary of Events and Information	Remarks and references to Appendices
Maidstone	Feby 9/16.		Anti aircraft observation post at LINTON established 1 N.C.O & 4 men	JB
	Feby 24.		The Battalion received orders to hold itself in readiness to move in case of alarm	JB

[Signature] Lieut. Colonel,
Commanding
2/4 Bn. 2a Lancashire Regiment.